I QUESTION, THEREFORE I AM!

Saifuddin Kamran

First published in 2021 in Australia

But Why?

What next?

What if?

Why should I do this?

What if I fail?

What if I succeed?

Ask questions. Answer questions. Answering questions helps one to understand about ourselves. It might expose one to see the absurdity of some desires by creating a better picture in term of the consequences of those desires being met. Or it might make one serious about doing something to minimize the negative effects of something that can happen. Or it might make one a careful person in some aspects of life. In most cases, thinking about a possible event, its consequences, the possible solutions, etc. makes one less worried about the event. This is what I call the Worst Case Scenario method. What is the worst that can happen? That's it.

Let us answer these questions now. No need to answer them all or to do the activity in any order. The idea is to make one think.

While answering, try to break these into more sub-questions like:

- Is it a good thing or bad thing to happen?
- What is the worst consequence?
- What can I do to lessen the negative consequences?
- What can I do to increase these in my life?
- Whom I can go to for guidance? etc.

EXISTENTIAL

What if I die suddenly tomorrow?

What if I am told that I have only a week to live?

What if were an animal, bird, stone, tree?

What if I could fly?

What if there is just this life and nothing after that?

What if the next life is better than this one?

____

____

____

____

____

____

____

____

____

____

____

____

What if I can see what others cannot?

What if all religious leaders were charlatans or didn't know themselves the whole story?

What if I could go back in time and do time travel?

What is the worst that can happen to me?

What if I could see what will happen after ten years, twenty years?

OCIAL

What is really stopping me from doing what I want to do?

What if I lose my best friend?

What if I meet someone today who will change me?

What if I lost all the material wealth I had?

____

____

____

____

____

____

____

____

____

____

____

____

Do people like me? Do I really want people to like me? What can I do to make them like me?

What I will do if I know nobody is watching?

What makes me happy? What can I do to increase my happiness?

What if I contract a disease that nobody is allowed to come close to me?

What if I am accused of a false charge?

What makes me sad? How I can avoid these?

____

____

____

____

____

____

____

____

____

____

____

____

What if I lose my memory?

What if I win a lottery?

What makes me angry? How can I avoid such situations?

____

____

____

____

____

____

____

____

____

____

____

____

What if I get the job I had been praying for?

What if I earn a lot of money in my business in a short time?

What if I move to new city, a new country?

What if I change my profession?

What if I am fired from the company?

What if I learn a new skill?

What if my boss has a crush on me?

____

____

____

____

____

____

____

____

____

____

____

____

What if I am involved in a car accident?

What if I could really marry the person I always wanted to?

PHYSIOLOGICAL

What if I lose my eyesight?

What if I lose a limb?

What if I become bedridden because of an accident or disease?

What if I lose my ability to speak?

What if I lose my ability to listen?

What if I gain a lot of weight?

What if I attain a beautiful body because of exercise or a better diet, etc.?

What if I lose my face to a terrible disease or accident?

What if I am able to change my gender?

What if I am able to gain a lot of strength because of exercise or diet, etc.?

What if I lose my appetite?

What if I am put on a restricted diet?

What if I am able to walk or cycle long distances?

BUSINESS

What if I succeed in my business?

____

____

____

____

____

____

____

____

____

____

____

What if I lose all my investment?

What if customers love my product?

What if customers reject the product I have spent a fortune on to develop and market?

What if the lifestyle changes and my product is of no use anymore?

What if the product I developed becomes one of the best inventions of recent times?

____

____

____

____

____

____

____

____

____

____

____

____

What if I am sued for damages because of some product failures?

What if I become known in the field I am working in?

What if a successful competitor takes away most of my customers?

What if I reduce the price?

What if I increase the price?

What if I am able to source the product or the raw material at very low prices?

What if I lose my best workers?

What if I am able to hire a great workforce?

What if I get more orders than I could supply?